An
Indian
Affair

Anil Pathak

To Ash
with love

Anil
X.

Anil Pathak

Booktrail Agency
8838 Sleepy Hollow Rd.
Kansas City, MO 64114
www.booktrail-agency.com

Publisher's Note: This is a work of fiction. Names, characters, places, and incidents are a product of the author's imagination. Locales and public names are sometimes used for atmospheric purposes. Any resemblance to actual people, living or dead, or to businesses, companies, events, institutions, or locales is completely coincidental.

An Indian Affair/ Anil Pathak
ISBN 978-1-7328704-7-5

Contents

An Indian Affair

On Graduating

Jai had just graduated. The year was 1993 during the month November. It was as though the last four years of his life had been for nothing as he had only a poor honours degree in Civil Engineering to show for it.

Jai was disappointed. But he knew that in his final year he had not participated in the lectures he was supposed to attend. Instead of attending lectures, his life for the last two years of his degree was spent in work for a security company and in binge drinking and drug taking.

At the time of his graduation, he was living with people who took L.S.D and cocaine just to get through each day. That didn't help him. But in his heart, he wanted to get his degree to show his family, especially his father, that he could do it. That he could accomplish something even though pursuing a career in Civil Engineering was not part of his intentions. He wanted to be an artist. An abstract artist. He had a talent in drawing portraits. He had already accomplished drawings including those of top Hollywood and Bollywood actors and actresses.

But Jai was insecure in himself. He had no real friends. No one he could talk to apart from his friend called Tom and Isabella, Tom's girlfriend. Both who would come over occasionally and participate in the taking of drugs, mainly smoking hemp and cannabis. They were old friends whom he had met at college while he was in Nottingham in 87' 88'. They would listen to Dylan and his album *'Desire'* while they got stoned. Tom would talk of his love for the Dutch and Isabella was hurt by this due to the fact that she knew that Tom was seeing someone else.

Tom knew that Jai knew this, and he did suspect that Isabella knew this also. But it didn't deter him as in both Jai's and Isabella's eyes, they knew him as a free spirit a bit like themselves really, but Isabella still didn't like it as he talked of moving to the Netherlands when he finished his degree in Urban Studies. Isabella was a rich man's daughter who could be described as a socialite. A very pretty Italian girl in appearance and at the time, young at the age of 20 years unfortunately she suffered from asthma and she still would smoke a joint as if she didn't have it. She was very quiet for a socialite and she wouldn't say much during the times that all three of them had spent together.

And so, after graduating, Jai would continue working as a security guard in prestigious working environments including the Communications Building in the centre of London. He was working twelve hours every day as he was in debt with his landlord owing back rent and to drug dealers who were constantly chasing him for money. He was in no hurry to return to his family home in Nottingham as he also owed money to some dubious characters there as well.

The other reason, more like the main reason, for not wishing to return home was his father who he had great animosity for. Jai would often take motorcycles and go for long rides through central London (as he had just past his motorcycle test in Nov 92) and into the country and dump them in some obscure place in the countryside returning home by hitchhiking thinking about his father and what he had put him through in his childhood years through to his early adult life. But little did Jai know, there was more to come.

The years (from 1993) past quickly Jai was always reminded of his insecurities by his alter ego, which would take control of his self when he became down on himself and therefore depressed to a point that he wouldn't go out for lengthy durations, stay in his room which was in a house that he shared with his drug taking colleagues he would read books on the psychology of the mind for which he had little understanding off, he would constantly be in a battle of trying to reassure himself that he wasn't going mental, he would often steal motorcycles again and again and go for long journeys out of town to places along the coast like Great Yarmouth and Sussex he would visit arcades and the gaming machines within them losing and making money so as to pass the time in what he saw was a hopeless life in the pursuit of pleasure that he undeniably craved for on the beaches of Great Yarmouth he would meet bikers of various gangs who he befriended and kept contact with during his extended stay in Essex where he dwelled. He would go to bars at night and see pitiful gangs of bikers brawl and argue over pathetic disagreements that they seemed to have with each other night after night after night. Jai became bored with this he longed for something new to touch upon his life to give his alter ego a break and to lift him where cocaine couldn't. His drug habits grew experimenting with crack cocaine heroin and other barbiturates that in the end did drive him to distraction extreme emotive feelings and an obsession for love with someone which he never had in his life. Jai in his drunken stupor was a mess, he spoke incoherently most of the time to people who he didn't even know that well he had put himself in a dangerous position and inside he knew it.

Spending nights out of his mind on cold unwelcoming beaches with only his leather jacket for warmth he would think on his life as an introverted child, teenager and young man purely due to his unrelenting father.

He could remember the events of his childhood which would haunt him forever, the times when he needed love and understanding and there was none to be found.

Revlo

Revlo was a gang member of a biker group who sympathised with Jai. They would at times leave the others behind and ride south into obscure country where they would talk on Jai's past and the events from that time which had haunted Jai. Revlo became a close and reliable friend to Jai.

Revlo, also as *'The Revolver'*, was an American Indian from Los Angeles who was well equipped with an excellent physique and sharp mind. He was a man who, despite his time spent behind bars for murder, was a relentless force to Jai. A person that Jai would turn to in times of dire need and support, he introduced him to Sam a pretty biker chick who would sometimes hang with them as they took to the road for comfort.

Jai found out that they were involved together but that time had passed, and she was looking for a new mate which consequently she found in Jai. Jai had got to learn of her life full of abuse and disregard from those who were supposed to be close to her throughout her upbringing but turned out of be, well birds of a different feather.

Sam, (short for Sammy) was around 5.9", 20 years of age with a mysterious character bronzed all over with sky blue eyes.

Jai had forgotten his life in London, Essex for a time while he spent more and more time with Revlo and Sam.

Revlo often talked about his life's history with strong reference to his battered and bruised relations with relatives all from more or less the same tribe of Indians who grew up in the mountains of Nevada Revlo was 37 years of age, a man graced with good lucks and an unfortunate scar which ran from his left cheek up to his forehead from a knife fight.

"When you were alone and sought comfort from those around you where did it come from? Jai replied, with Sam in toe.... to God and his disciples who Jai thought had forgotten him in his time of need.... but he still believed.... believed in hope and he read a poem that he wrote to both Revlo and Sam the poem was called hope Revlo frowned with a hint of laughter but then he said, "let's hear it ...." and Jai recited:

<u>"Hope",</u>

I wander slowly through tall trees

I am the shoulders of a light winter breeze

I am the sound all diminishing

I see you cry all alone

I am the want in your tearful eyes

I am the light in a summer's sunshine

I am the bite of the night's, come to me please

I could bring you down to your knees.

I am in the hills as you stare

But I am good, I can never catch your unawares!

Be comforted, for I am there

Revlo stood up and gave Jai a standing ovation Sam was watching with a thoughtful expression. "I didn't know you were a poet" "Not were Jai explained, "I still am" Sam said "Whoa, it's beautiful, can I hear it again?" and Jai recited it. Again, Revlo announced that in jail he was also a practising poet, then he recited a couple of his,

Run River, My Beauty Run.

These rivers are clean

These waters are far from seen

I shan't tell you the places, I have been

I can't explain the waste lands in a dream

Into the water we do go

as we hear the tractor travelling by slow

The experienced river as it holds you in a swim

glimmering mellow from the corner of your eye

as one reaches to the end of the green hilly bank

leaving a trail of water drenched feet

feels so great as you attempt a joyous leap!!

The Native Indian.

They had to fight with one thought, to win

as time grew heavy, their fight grew thin

once a roaring lion, to a sickly din

But the Indian, the Indian will not die!!

Even if they talk from way up in the sky.

For they will sing you to sleep

and wipe away your weep

Into your soul they will creep

and with you, they will lie deep

until the light fills your eyes from the sun in your

skies

Now the tracker will not have his day

because the tracking is all but done

Soundly he will not sleep

For in his memory it will be shown

that time will never leave him alone

for a pure heart with no hate or greed

will be the one to work for, as it is our only need!

"What do you think of that?" Revlo cried. "They were told to me by my father, and he knew what he was talking about when it came to the oppressed and despondent."

Sam came closer to Jai and they hugged and kissed for the second time they left Revlo by the fire on the beach with the bikes as Jai and Sam wandered further up the beach. They stopped and while Jai stroked her long black hair fondly, Sam kissed him gently on the lips Jai kissed her back "Your lips taste like strawberries," Jai muttered Sam smiled as she undid his leather jacket throwing it to the floor, both knelt down into the soft sand and they both caressed each other until both were lying there Jai was caressing her gently and undid her blouse, the movement was slow as they found themselves entwined in each other's arms the moment was bliss Jai slowly lifted up her skirt and played gently with her thighs and slowly undid his belt and buttons on his jeans she moaned softly as she felt him penetrating her with the love that she so needed from him as he was making love to her he gently caressed her erect nipples her lips were wet as was her clitoris as he wasted no time in pushing against her body again and again and again until she cried out slightly louder than she did before he moved his hands down her soft flowing back until he was caressing her buttocks and then he kept his mouth on her erect nipples sucking them until she came to her climax and her soft clitoris exploded with love juices Jai was harder than ever he rolled over onto the sand and Sam took him within her hands and gently moved them up and down up and down and then slightly faster then she caressed him until he came. The moment was exhilarating and sensuous they both continued to fondle each other, and they then rested after such a mouth-watering moment. They kissed each other so passionately and continued to fondle each other restlessly.

Revlo was stretched out by the fire at this time lighting a joint having just finished snorting two rather large lines of coke he was thinking about what Jai had said to him earlier that day regarding his father and how different he was to his own, who can only be described as the complete opposite to what he had heard from Jai The weather was pleasant with no breeze at all. All was still at around 10.45 pm Revlo remarked to himself that they were probably getting off together and he was happy for them and happy within himself as he opened his wallet and took out the picture of his beloved Katrina in her naked form.

A beautiful creature with a firm bronzed body and short blonde hair with flashing blue eyes and a cute smile.

He sucked on the joint as he saw Jai and Sam coming towards him. They were hand in hand smiling at Revlo as he took another thick line which was laid out on his black leather jacket beside him. Sam and Jai also settled beside the fire, breaking out some coke as they both took two large, ample lines. They laughed all together looking into the fire getting warm again. Jai would hang out with Sam his new-found love as he was directionless without her it seemed Revlo returned to his biker gang and said that he would be in touch.

Kensal Rise

Jai reached Essex again with the remembrance of the kiss that Sam had given him he wiped down the motorcycle leaving it in Central London Leicester Square somewhere and started working as a Security Guard at his usual place at the communications building after a few days at home in Essex.

Jai's mind was like an unstable temperature condition after a few days working he decided that he couldn't do security work no more he longed for Sam, but he knew she was also busy working in a law firm across London as a secretary.

He returned home after handing in his resignation he had enough money saved now to enjoy a quiet life and that is exactly what he did.

He would often visit his friend Mark, a law student in Kensal Rise where he shared a flat with a colleague. Mark was also from Nottingham and was in his final year at London University again he would sit and chat whilst enjoying cocaine and grass at their earliest convenience.

They would talk over their times in Nottingham whilst both at College, Bilborough College a time that really Jai wouldn't have minded forgetting. It was about that time where he was living at Karibu Youth hostel after leaving home, after a massive argument with his father.

Unfortunately, Mark was a reminder of that time, (not his fault), but they would just chill out and listen to albums of various sorts like soul funk and lots of Jazz together with The Doors, Janis Joplin and Pink Floyd. They would visit London (Central)

Kings road and Camden market not really buying much but visiting bars clubs at night and of course Ronnie Scotts.

Mark would take the micky out of Jai for not having a girlfriend and Jai would sarcastically say "Oh well. I forgot to get one."

Jai would take Mark on a motorcycle ride through Central London it was so easy to take a motorcycle in those days because most of them weren't alarmed. Well not the older ones anyway.

They would seldom talk about what they had got up to – the cocaine played a big part in that. It gave them (when they were together) a sense of escapism from everything, problems the mundane affairs of everyday disillusionment they basically talked about the music they were listening too the vibe of the living London the thrill of living in London and all those pretty girls who were there astoundingly beautiful, really up for it.

Jai and Mark along with Tracy, Mark's girl would go out and have a fantastic time. They (all three) would take a few lines each pop a pill and hit the town. There was one time where Jai was dancing on the floor of a prestigious London bar and he was pushed to the floor by this black guy the two ended up in a brawl and basically blood flowed and Mark joined in at that point they were all thrown out. After they had fixed themselves up with the help of Tracy who just happened to be a nurse, they went home inviting a few ladies who were waiting outside a club but couldn't get in for some reason and so all of them (five in total) were invited back to Mark's flat. Where after a little boogie in the sitting room they all agreed to have an orgy and so there they all stripped and fondled each other whilst in a drunken haze doped up on pills everyone participated and a great time was had by all especially Jai and Mark who were the lucky recipients of tender loving care and a lot more from six gorgeous women all in their twenties.

As Jai was snorting coke from Cindy's firm buttocks Mark was making love to Carol while the rest of the girls were licking and fondling each other there were moans and groans coming from the sitting room and it was all so fantastical. Carol was on top of Mark and she was riding him like a pro, Mark was in ecstasy clutching her smooth, 23 year old buttocks as she rode him, as she was slowly reaching a climax, Mark then took control and held her while he loved her from underneath her and within 35 secs she climaxed she got off Mark and started to fondle him with her mouth lovingly moving so slowly and gently that Mark was moaning and groaning at every movement that Carol made, Mark was in heaven with the coke he had taken which was kicking in more so than before Mark stroked Carol's hair removing it to one side from her eyes.

Jai at this time was making love to Cindy they were doing it doggy fashion holding on to her firm young tanned breasts he was making every stroke that he gave her, count. He could see the love juices flow out of Cindy, decorating Jai's body as Cindy cried out, "Yes! Please make love to me harder! Make love to me harder, please!" Jai obliged and in a matter of minutes Jai had come onto Cindy's firm buttocks. She turned to look at him, grabbed him and she slowly caressed him.

Cindy left with Jai, Mark was still sleeping when they left the flat. They travelled across London together stopping in a shop or two. Cindy was a librarian she was brought up in London and she worked at the University of London's Main library, she was quite a shy girl as Jai got to know her better through their journey, she was quite petite and had a beautiful body, pretty complexion and shiny green eyes.

"What's your ideal girl like?" she uttered, to Jai, Jai replied "you are" she smiled and gave him a parting big kiss they exchanged numbers and addresses, then they parted company. It was the end of 1995 and Jai was in trouble with all his insecurities.

Jai's predicament in 1996

Jai knew that all this had to come to an end, that is, the womanising the binge drinking the cocaine, along with the regular trips, (L.S.D), that he was taking it all had to stop. He was 26 years old and with grave concerns about his future.

He had decided to write an account a true synopsis of himself and this commenced in 1996 and he started with an honest account of his background his animosity towards his father and the trip to India that was agreed by all, (his family and himself that he would embark on with in the year of 1996) would be the best thing that he could do to ignite his career, despite his concerns with his family.

Whilst in India he would remember all that would go on and engrave it in his mind and if for any reason the trip didn't work out for him, he would write a full account of his stay in India why he could not stay there and all together with his thoughts and fears whilst in India. He would document all of this in his mind and in writing, as he knew that he would be sent out there on condition that he would travel with a single airline ticket and not a return. He was therefore aware of the pitfalls and that it would be difficult, very difficult to convince his parents to send him a return ticket. Knowing all of this he would commence the whole initial synopsis in his mind, together with the actual event itself and it goes as follows: -

A

Brief History of Jai's

Background

The day dawned when it was time to think about my career as a Civil Engineer while I was in London.

Previously I had received a phone call from my sister, who asked me to give up my hopeless life in London to pursue a career in India, to therefore gain experience in Civil Engineering so as (in a number of years) to gain sufficient experience so that I might be in a position to apply for posts in the UK.

My life in London spanned for approximately six years, those years including the four years it took me to graduate with a Civil Engineering Honours Degree with a pass as a result, of those four years.

It was apparent to me at the time of graduating in November 1993, that I would not after countless applications to various consultancies and contractors that I would not secure gainful employment in the profession I'd chosen.

I therefore embarked on two years or so (after graduating) in a life of hard drinking and drug taking, to numb the pain of my previous failures that is in not securing a good degree. I had developed a drinking habit and cocaine habit, which had kept me busy whilst at university (the latter part of the course) to the end of 1995.

My parents were not pleased with my current disposition, obviously. Their knowledge of my binge drinking and drug taking where not made aware to them, as far as I was aware.

Whilst at university I also worked weekends and summer holidays where I had sufficient funds to pay for my drugs and drinking habits.

I had quickly come to the realisation that it was time for a change, in me and that of my circumstance, if I was to have any chance of a career at all.

I had a problem with my left eye caused by a penetrating injury at the tender age of five, in the mid-seventies, 1975 to be exact. I had constant permanent double vision and my vision without aids was impaired severely. This in itself had confined me to a state of irreversible depression and anxiety (conditions of which I still suffer from) as the symptoms of low self-esteem and severe lack of confidence grew, my mind was in a constant battle of reassurance that I had tried to give myself and the paranoia that I was constantly fighting within myself. As a result of the above, ultimately, I was in constant turmoil (that is my mind was in constant turmoil) and happiness and contentment escaped me ever since I was a child.

These were the main reasons for my delving into a constant search for escapism, which I found in taking proscribed drugs, which for a number of years were welcomed, very much so, by myself.

My upbringing was very conservative as my father was, he never took the time to question my feelings or emotions, he was only interested in results, as he often pointed out to me. He was a tyrant. As I was the only son I was expected to do well in my studies at school and through further education.

I was expected to rise a 5 O'clock in the mornings go for a long run and be back in time, to revise what

I had learnt at school, the previous week which I was duly tested on at every weekend and school holidays this was my life for a good four years, whilst I was at school. I frequently got the answers wrong, for which I was chastised with words and shouting anger from my father.

I had come out of my teenage years battered and bruised with feelings of hate and anguish and dislike towards my father, the world and it nearly broke me and my fragile mind, at the age of seventeen I had decided to leave home which I don't think my mother ever forgave me for. I returned home after some time spent at the Karibu Youth Hostel at the later part of my eighteenth year, to study for my 'A Levels' which I had failed, so from there I was given a chance by the University of East London to study six HND units in Civil Engineering (in order for me to get onto the first year of the honours degree course), which I had passed in 1989 so I thus commenced the 3 year degree course in 1990.

The Journey

The feelings I had were mixed and various whilst I thought about embarking on a journey that I hoped would shape the rest of my life.

I put a lot of trust into my parents in terms of the living accommodation that I would receive, the feelings of hopeful wellbeing that I would have in the persons whom were to be my companions (whom although strangers to me, were related to my family and I).

But I was told that I would be spending at least five years in India, New Delhi, with my uncle and aunt and so would embark on the journey with no return ticket but just a single one to India, New Delhi. Again, I had put a lot of trust in my family in that if it didn't work out in Delhi, I would be assured that they would send me a return ticket, so that I may return to England. I was secretly indisposed and therefore reluctant to go without a return ticket for I had no idea that my father would make me suffer out there and make me literally beg for a return ticket. This thought of deception a cruel deception anchored on my mind for some time after I was made aware that I would be travelling with only a single ticket to New Delhi.

I know that feelings of pride and just in what I was setting out to achieve, to ultimately make my life, reassured me and the delight that my family had shown in my making the what they felt and what I felt was the right decision to embark on this journey made, put to the back of my mind any ideas of betrayal in not sending me a return ticket, as and when needed. But I could not help but believe that something could go wrong in respect to the way my father was, in terms of the experiences I had already shared with him in the earlier years of my upbringing. For example, when I was a teenager, I commenced employment as a waiter in a prestigious restaurant and my wages were taken by my father his reason being that he had more need of them than I had.

I could not argue the fact because I was living under his roof and also as a child of 12, 13 and 14 my father mother and I would work on the markets selling electrical goods at Watnall Market in Nottingham where I would wake at around 4.45 am to prepare to work and travel to the markets which was as I remember some distance away from home at the weekends.

I was never paid for the work that I did. Again, I could not argue the fact of not being paid as I was living under his roof. I had developed a real animosity for my father as I also had to take on jobs around the house of putting up fencing painting and decorating and many other tasks through the years being at 10 years old through to when I left home. Whilst a child and through my teenage years he would not allow me to go swimming with my friends at school, or, college parties or clubbing at all throughout my upbringing.

With these thoughts in mind and with the animosity that I felt towards him I would agree to go to Delhi and do what was seen all round as the right thing to do. Even though the sun had disappeared from my life long ago.

As I looked through the coach window looking at the scenery as we drove, I didn't feel anything; not excited or a thrill of any kind, but, numb. I enjoyed the scenery, but I was pleased to be on my own and London was sensational to look at as we arrived at our destination.

My Sister and her husband met me at Heathrow and I was happy to see them. The plane ride was one that would go on for ever it was a means to an end. I thought what the hell have I got myself into.

I knew New Delhi was well known for poverty and oppression as I remembered a trip made at the age of 11 years, remembering giving all my rupees that I had in my possession. Coming out of the Airport greeted by the oppressed and poor in rags and faces that were lost and full of torment and isolated to the hilt.

Finally, however my eyes were in India, New Delhi and somehow it was the same as I imagined it would be, with new sights like half a man in a cart like contraption using his arms accelerating slowly along the road, buses motorcycles and cars waiting in the traffic the smell of a thousand scents, as I met with my uncle, we greeted and then went on our way through the large areas of arid ground with lots of signs of life there, the vastness of the place, the marketeers sitting on their market stalls or on the floor, smoking and looking at passers-by, the road was bumpy and as I thought there were few traffic signs.

We arrived at the Colony where there were blocks of apartments and a small park, nearby. I had finally arrived at the dwelling which was to be my home for the next four months. The apartment was a one bedroom flat where there was my uncle and aunt and their small, two small children, two boys, whom I greeted.

I couldn't believe it as I sat down thinking that I was to share the sitting room floor with the two boys, this would be the place where I would sleep I had always thought that my uncle with his job as a Branch Manager at the Punjab National Bank would off lived a little better, but as I found out later he had made some bad investments and he was living hand to mouth. His wife also worked at a Government post. I couldn't believe that my father had sent me here. I was angry and humiliated to think that I was expected to sleep on the floor with my uncles (Sunil) two young sons in the sitting room area which was the only place where I could sleep, I was in a state of shock, but I kept mum as I didn't want to upset my new-found relatives.

The Betrayal

The first night was horrific it was sweltering all through the day and night and the electricity in the whole Colony would frequently just cut out and the a/c would stop working together with the lights and the overhead fans.

Lizards and rats were a common feature there were no mosquito nets and I was repeatedly bitten and the rats and lizards which were about the size of a man's hand would dart about, up the walls, flying over my head whilst I was trying to sleep.

After two or close to two weeks of this I had had enough, really, it was too much to cope with. I was dumb founded and felt betrayed by my next of kin, my animosity grew. I had made Sunil uncle aware of this and he listened to my concerns and the reasons why I couldn't hope to work and live under these conditions.

I wrote a strong letter to my father conveying all that was going on and he said that if I wanted to return to England then I would have to work to earn the money for a return ticket.

I was very disappointed. My mind was about to blow, but somehow, I pulled myself together, I wandered if this whole deal had been planned – a conspiracy. But I couldn't prove a damned thing! I felt that this was a lesson, thrusted upon me by my father. The feelings of terror and betrayal were all common to me. The dream, I thought, was a nightmare in disguise. What joy I felt, once greeting Sunil's Uncle and his family, poured out of me, like tipping water from a cup. I thought, what the Hell have I stepped into, poverty and oppression which to me together with the environment and weather conditions was pollution. I was isolated, I felt as if I was thrown on a dung heap, discarded like a piece of something...... and I wasn't given the chance to change. That is in the right surroundings, i.e. a bed or even a mattress and somewhere where I could shower daily. Water was a problem in this Colony. Some days there wasn't enough water to wash and shower with.

I really felt that I was a victim of the third world with even the basic essentials being a mystery to me.

During the Stay :

The Awakening

During my time in India I witnessed people in more desperate circumstances than myself.

I went to a large market called South-ex, there I saw people along the roadside sleeping, begging in torn clothing dirty and at some intervals the stench was so putrid and overbearing that I was quite sick at times. The rickshaws were plentiful in and around the market. There were open sewers in the streets and again bad smells from all around. New Delhi was indeed a place of high pollution, with the increased population, the swarms of dogs that were just so malnourished, it was very difficult for me not to feel sorry for them. There was one time I hurdled some bread to a dog and the next thing I knew as I turned, there were at least 50 or 60 dogs suddenly appearing looking straight at me waiting to follow me, my auntie was behind me scared stiff and all I could do was throw stones at them hoping that they would disengage and leave my aunt and me alone. This was achieved after about five minutes, of throwing stones in their direction and we were at peace again.

At evening times when Sunil returned from the office we would sometimes go to see some of his friends, where I was left to defend myself, they, well, most of Sunil's friends thought that I had to explain my shortcomings i.e. why I wouldn't stay in India and work I was astonished and felt angry and self-conscious that they would talk as if I had shortcomings to answer for, I was in an unbelievable position. I felt confounded and then I had to explain my way, each step of the way. I could not believe their rudeness and disbelief that they were taking sides against me, although a few of his friends had some sympathies with me and I was able to express freely objections that I felt in staying, Sunil also showed some sympathy with the predicament, I found myself in.

At times I would wander slowly to the nearby shop and purchase cigarettes and processed cheese and bread, the cheese came in a tin! I would then go to the nearby park and take a round before going back to the Colony. Solace was not part of the package on this trip, but somehow, I remained calm mostly with my dignity intact.... but it was very hard at times. At times I thought that I was losing my mind it seemed that my family had turned against me and that I had very few sympathies. Inside I was truely devastated But I had never known so much of a rush of sound around my ears as this India was, I was so swamped

by it.

The Philosophy

Every day was a battle to stay together in myself and not give way to despair.

Thoughts of despair marrying sorrow were not new to me, it always led me to one path in the past during those years after finishing my studies – drugs and drink none of which could cure my human condition during my times of what seemed like confinement to the Colony and to its immediate surroundings.

I longed for England for London, where I had left many friends.

I would write poems and ones that stuck with me in particular were:

A Poem for the Hopeless.

I live in the past there's no question

It seems like a test, there is compassion

My fears they awake me

Some days I am lost in myself and can't do battle

It's true, I'm cross, because I fall out of the saddle

But as they say, there's hope in every little way

Hope in every little day.

I'm sure it will pass as it travels along its way.

Life – one world to another.

Isn't life a wonderous place?

Isn't life a beautiful place?

Isn't it should I say a pitiful place?!

Isn't life a brutal unforgiving place?

Isn't life a beautiful place?

Isn't life a warm and sweet-smelling place?!

Isn't life a filthy and dirty place?!

Isn't life a wonderful place?!

Some say yes, Some say nothing, Some say maybe

and some say something

half the world says what they say

and the other half say what they say

half the world struggle to live and half

the world drink until they sway

Isn't life a beautiful thing!!!

The Revolution

We believe because we are disillusioned

We die because we are lost

We fight because we are afraid

We lose because we just have got nothing left

We live for the revolution

long live the revolution

whatever your revolution maybe

The Hated

The time for hate is done

The hater, what will he become?

because in his heart he carries the cold

which is all he knows, what a waste of a soul

but no, as he has no soul, then there is none to be
wasted

His journey will end as miserably as it started

His life is already over....

as he lived it he has never reached for a cure

what a sad, sad affair for one who could never live

with the words to be fair

all I can see is despair despair

what a nightmare, for those who don't really care!

Storm

Storm in the night

Dare you dance in its sight?

storm in the night

what do you think as it shows you its might?!

Does it make you strong as it sings its song?

Or does it smash your insides, as it reaches down

from the skies

I hope you feel the storm I know

and that it reaches you with a positive glow.

Find it.... somewhere!

Love is the force that will bind us

trouble may one day find us

It may become a test that will challenge us

But we will prosper in the time that God gave us.

I know not what life has in store

but I know now that love is something one does

not have to endure.

So, love in the first and love in the last

that's a way, to beat the demons at last.

There were many more that lead me to a positive sphere and ones that, yes, did leave me astray. But I kept them to myself as it was, (not meaning to sound selfish) myself that I was ultimately trying to help and my soul which within those impossible days and weeks, to save.

The Bridge to Far

There was a temple in some obscure place that for the life of me cannot remember the place where we were destined. We were following, in a taxi, Sunil's younger brother, (Satish), we reached a long and straight bridge we travelled at around 5.30 am and so this part of the journey seemed peaceful, even though there was traffic. Unfortunately, Sunil's brother, Satish, had met with an accident, his scooter was there a few yards from where he was lying. His hands were shaking and covered in blood, as was part of his face. The rest of the party decided to go on to the nearest hospital leaving me with him. There was no shelter on the bridge and so after about 40 minutes, there came a shower of some vigour. Satish was taken of too hospital by that time and I was left with the scooter. I was told that someone would collect both the scooter and me. I waited in the rain, that unforgiving rain for 3 hours and 25 minutes before someone came in a lorry. Satish, I heard later was alright just shell shocked with cuts and bruises to his face arms and lower legs.

I was taken back home. After about 1 hour, we reached the Colony and there I had the worst fever, I had ever had, this illness was so bad. I lay for close to four days, it reminded me of a time when I had contracted Tuberculosis as a child I just had to lay there and sweat it out. I was ok after four long days of basically constant shivering.

After some time, a few weeks at least I noticed that I had lost weight at least 2 stones. I had no appetite to eat their rich food even the daal was spiced with a rich masala. So, I survived on sweet bread and processed cheese and water. I was given no medication but two paracetamols whilst ill.

I had no faith in god by that time and I felt that this was the reason why we never made that journey. I would off only been interested in the building itself, anyway, the architecture.

I thought that these who were supposed to be close relatives paid very little attention to me whilst I was there with them in New Delhi. I thought that they were related to my father as they had the same air of coldness and almost resentment towards me. In hindsight I could see this, and it was everything but comforting. I tried to pay it little mind and kept mum, for the duration.

London, England

After several letters it was seen that my family's mission to make me work was conclusive as a failed attempt.

On the 20th of July 1996, I had finally received a letter with sufficient funds to purchase a return ticket, to England.

The suffering or should I say the grave suffering was nearly over.

I can remember quite vividly that while I was shaving, I had taken off a rather expensive watch, when I returned to retrieve it, it had vanished, but, no matter, I was soon to leave this awful place and I had made sure that my goodbyes were of little consequence.

I had lost so much weight that I can safely say that I was half the man I used to be. Even the watch which had been with me for five years, had no real effect on me as I had been most deviously played as a fool, the thing that hurt the most was that I was sure it was a conspiracy a joint conspiracy between my immediate family and my so-called relatives.

I returned home feeling as little as I could make myself to feel.

When I arrived at Nottingham to my family home I had only one problem that gauged me, this was of course, how to get away from my family.

I moved out to a flat as soon as was possible in Nottingham.

After India

Jai then spent the next 10 months working as an assistant manager in Retail with a company called Topfloor Clothing where he would save enough to establish himself once again in his beloved city of London.

Jai had moved in to his new flat, 3 weeks ago. His mind was everywhere, but mainly his mind was frustrated and angry bearing new scars to which he didn't want, or, had time for. But he took solace in the fact that he was once again in London which he had ached for and that he was working in retail once again.

He didn't know what plans he had (long term plans) but even he consoled himself that it was too early to have plans he had that expectation of himself to which trait his father had embossed on his mind through their time together, oh how he hated him to not allow him to be himself, he felt anything but laid back and happy but he decided that it was natural for him to feel this way and elation would be a long time coming, but he had to get it together as he had just taken on a new post as an assistant manager at Top floor clothing. He had only been there a week and then he scored some coke of Revlo who had said a visit was imminent from him.

After work on Friday 29th July 1997 he popped into "the three features' an up and coming wine bar he spent an hour there before his return home.

At home he would drink more and wondered what he would do this weekend as he had time off work, he thought about going out on the town, but he was too tired for that then, he thought about a hooker. He would stay in alone call Revlo and hopefully he would bring some friends with him.

Revlo arrived with two female friends they sat and talked for a while about India and Jai felt that not even a night on the town, or 1000 nights on the town could not relinquish the rage he felt about the whole messy affair in India. Julie and Harriet listened as did Revlo with complete astonishment at what they were listening too.

After 2 grams of coke the four set out to Camden Market it was a Sunday, so the market was in bloom. The open market was astonishing so many things to buy in this beautiful part of London. Where the view of people was so cosmopolitan.

Jai saw a lot more in this market then he was to expect, all the Cafe's and places in alleys astonished him. He could spend his whole month's salary on just one visit. The scrumptious foods and the many types of tobacco's that he'd noticed at various tobacconists around, the funky clothes shops of varying kinds. The furniture shops of antiquated retro seventies, sixties and of the newest kinds, together with the sweet aroma of the Wandering Skies really captivating the imagination, he had flashbacks of South-ex in New Delhi but Camden Market was a lot cleaner a lot less pollution. The streets looked like a combed head of hair compared to South-ex.

Jai was still conscious stricken Harriet and Julie were looking at a clothes stall Revlo was with them Jai just had to go he made his excuses to his friends and went along the Camden lock to meet his dealer he purchased 2 grams of coke and some grass then went on his way towards Romford in Essex.

Jai just couldn't get the events, previous out of his mind and how cruelly he had been treated by his family. He was upset that all this dawned on him whilst in his favourite part of London, Camden Town. On arrival at home Revlo phoned asking how he was and that he was hoping for all four of them to have a celebration for Jai's arrival back to the U.K, Jai was still just not in the mood he kindly declined and said his good byes to Revlo "Until the next time Jai," said Revlo, "until the next time, my friend, try not to get too upset over India, your father just wanted the best for you, try to understand Jai," said Revlo.

Jai sat back down and opened a new bottle of Baileys along with a bottle of Cognac and whiskey, he then proceeded to open a bag of coke and prepared a line for himself, he then took a shot of whiskey followed by a little Bailey's to mask the taste of the whiskey. Scott and McKay his most favourite of brands of whiskey. He looked at the bottle and realised he was no happier than he was before he set out to India, but he was relieved that he was back in London, so very relieved.

Of course, his father didn't want to know how Jai really felt he just saw him as a failure and shunned him as a result. An unforgiving nature... yes, that was his father, Jai thought so in touch with his own feelings but no sympathy's with Jai's feelings. This was the reason for Jai's misery, but he wasn't going to fall into the trap of feelings of self-loathing which is what his father wanted. Yes, that trick of bringing Jai up in order for him to think just that, after failure didn't quite work with Jai. Jai was happy about that At least that was one thing that could be celebrated, and Jai prepared himself two more large lines of cokc and another shot of whiskey.

Jai was happy for that moment. It felt like a victory between his father and him.

Jai didn't think that Revlo was taking sides, but it was so naive, Jai thought, that he would say something like that. Jai felt that Revlo was high and happy as normal and that he said those words as a quick and easy explanation of how he could explain the situation between his father and Jai. But Revlo just didn't understand because no matter how high he was Revlo wouldn't have said those words.

By then Jai was in a stupor, he had drunk (3/4's) three quarters of the Scott and McKay and half (1/2) the bottle of the Baileys the coke was all but gone and Jai refused to let his misery increase further so he took himself with the help of a taxi, to Soho.

The Brothel

By the time Jai had got there he was half way sober and remarkably in good spirits he dismissed his father's guile for him, for one night and continued with the merriments of the night as he entered the brothel of Madame Sising's where the man enjoyed the company of two beautiful girls. The place itself had been all too common to Jai's eyes it was beautiful and extravagant it looked like a Turkish harem There were velvet seated sofa's Persian carpets and many doors in a large room where girls were half naked the music was and could only be described as Rare Gove with a slight mix of Jazz in it. It set the scene for a long and memorable night. And it didn't cost Jai the earth either. Jai was very good with money he had always been. A trait which he thanked his father for Yes.... at least his father came through on a good one for a change, thought Jai. Yes, Jai contained his anxieties in the shape of a barrel. The walls contained dark and mysterious shadows which flickered like a candle in the wind the pictures and beauty of them lit the fragments of his imagination pictures of beautiful sumptuous naked women extravagantly laid out, on the floors and walls of this intense surrounding the detail of the candle stick holders of gold and silver shining with demanding certainty. In describing fortune was described in a single wave of the consciousness when describing this large room. A carefully thought out decoration. The girls were extremely well mannered in their see-through lingerie and they both took to Jai like a swan to water Madame Sising's was an underground den where one if not shown the interior could only but envisage the detail of it.

Jai kissed both girls passionately on the lips and neck as he strolled to the nearest of the numerous doors on entering the room was a spitting image of the larger room. "Come in darling rest here while I fetch you a drink," what will you have?" the girl spoke with a posh conservative dialect she sounded intelligent a woman of the world, so did the other girl who he found out was barely 22 years of age they both wore black and red lingerie high heels and very little jewellery. The blonde went to the drinks cabinet while Lucy tenderly kissed him gently on the mouth and Jai's left hand stroked her hair and face while the other hand was against her hip moving up slowly to the clips on her bra which he undid with ease, the blonde, Silvi, came back touching Jai's shoulder laid the drink down and fondled with his hair gently, sitting down on the Red Velvet Sofa lifting Jai's jacket of his shoulders and then Lucy undid Jai's shirt buttons and Silvi then took the shirt off him she kissed him on the back of his neck and gently touched and caressed his back while Lucy stroked his member as it grew hard very quickly, then Jai stood up and gave them both a large line of coke after breaking out a bag which he lifted from the top of his sock there was a beautiful silver tray on the table and the girls smiled at Jai and preceded to snort the two lines simultaneously Jai also took a line and then a drink of cognac. The girls also drank champagne which Jai poured for them there was very little talk "A toast ...... to the future." "To the future" Lucy and Silvi replied. All three laughed as if the future was well known to all three to be a continuation of their respective lives. They then took to the four poster and ravaged themselves in each other's physiques, until the hour and a half was done.

Jai left the establishment thinking that was the best money that he had spent in a long time (apart, from the coach fare, from, Heathrow airport to Nottingham, previously). Jai had managed to obtain the phone number of Silvi and he had promised her a day out in London where he would dine with her and just have a catch-up. Jai must have had a lasting impression on her.

The Falling

A fortnight later Jai had contacted Silvi and they agreed to meet at Camden Lock for dinner. They met Silvi, who really knew how to carry herself in this lovely dinner suit she wore with her beautiful flowing blonde hair. "Lucy sends her kind regards," she explained as they kissed and sat down to a table at Fannucci's, a famous place in Camden. Jai smiled and sent his regards in kind.

Jai and Silvi both ordered pasta and the meal was delightful. Jai couldn't help but tell her of his past experience in India, Silvi listened intently. Silvi's upbringing was also rather conservative with middle class parents and a strict but alcoholic ridden father, that's why she explained, she had to get away from Devonshire, her place of birth. Jai totally understood where Silvi was coming from she had no hatred towards her family though and she was living a happy life working part time at Madame Sising's whilst studying for a psychology degree at London University.

Silvi explained to Jai how he could ground himself that is too keep him once grounded is to be in the here and now. Not anywhere else. Jai had heard of this technique but had never practised it on himself for some strange reason.

She explained further "the idea is to think of 5 smells you can smell and five things you can see and to always do this exercise when you find your mind wandering in other directions i.e. into other places and try not to do so much coke as this has psychotic tendencies, or symptoms."

Jai explained that the coke which when used quite frequently gave him a feeling of escapism from the past, the near past that he was finding it so difficult to forget. Silvi sympathised with his predicament and thought to herself that he wouldn't be doing coke if in fact, he didn't need it. Although she only took it for recreational purposes, she thought that it was a struggle for him.

Jai travelled through the next few weeks in a daze the barrel had broken, and all his anxieties came out. His work at Topfloor clothing had started to suffer, grounding, himself, just didn't seem to work. He had tried to paint to draw as he used too but nothing could excite him not art poetry or women not even his closest friends, Sam and Revlo. His job lasted for the next few months then he just crumbled like a broken biscuit His coke habit was getting worse his drinking excessive to say the least he had lost 1 ½ stone in so many months.

Jai had no word from his family either it was like he was left alone to face the hardships of life once, again. With no job he confined himself to his flat, only going out when he needed too the landlord was very understanding of his situation and let him claim for benefits to pay his rent. He was drained off energy and self-worth it looked very dark for Jai and at the wrong time, coming up to Christmas Jai once again was living quite alone like a hermit it seemed.

Months and months had passed, and Jai had got word from his sister that his father had died of a brain tumour. Jai cried like a baby upon the news he felt his life was falling apart he travelled to Nottingham for the cremation. The day was 9th Day of September 1998 when his father was cremated. Jai couldn't handle the stress of it all and went back to London on the 29th Sept.

Jai became lost and gave in to despair, but he would never forgive his father for what he did and

so, after Jai had settled in London once again, some
poems came to mind:

To The Defeated

Be now defeated

make sure the bed you lie in is Sheeted

Be now your friend insecure

For you should now know, how it feels now to be
intimidated

you cannot now go back.

its far out of track

Be yours on to yourself

Do not forget the Self

as you have done

consider your thoughts

Set sail again leaving all ports.

The Highwayman

Winter sings a dreary song

To one who walks all day long

on the highways of whichever city he dwells

around his neck rings the song of the two bells,

walking drunk, muttering slow

he fears not of friend or foe.

Smoke? Well there's a thought

I'll leave these streets, he says one day

I'll build a cabin where there's enough for two to lay

He still waits for his dreams to be fulfilled

as he mumbles .... when my head is clear

I'll be far from here, I'll be far from here

You'll see, you'll see, my dear, you'll see.......

when my head is clear........

Not wanting

I want no more, for the love, I bare

I seek no more solace in despair

cradle me in your friendship, so be there

find fortune in reason to be fair

crimson trees grow out there

a mooring birth I too do declare

for I am not finished, to this I'm fully aware

this day is not done, unfinished business, I swear.

About the book

Jai was once a happy go lucky character but unfortunately, he was directionless.

This book tells the story of Jai as a graduate and the hedonistic lifestyle that pursued him until he couldn't see to clearly anymore.

Jai's past would hit him hard in his mind and soul and it seemed that whatever he would do in life there really was no help for it. He was indeed haunted by the past and he constantly felt the need of escapism which he did in his pursuit of proscribed drugs drink and women.

This insight into Jai's life describes the incidents that occurred and the emotional impact that they had.

About the Author

In the Summer's breeze, there was no one more at ease than Anil Pathak.

In his way of learning there was no one more disconcerting than his right winged father.

And this thorn in his side from an early age took him on a stage far deeper than the depths of rage and there he stayed as his father swayed close by him.

And now he's gone the terrible mist went on and on and on through the life before him.

Anil Pathak graduated with an (Honours) Degree in Civil Engineering from the University of East London, in 1993.

His work The Sensuous Truth published in December 2016 as well as his latest offering An Indian Affair reflects the emotions and feelings of today's people and describes himself as a creator and master of his own destiny. He is a keen Poet and Artist. He resides in Brighton, England which is a Constant Inspiration to him, when creating his work.

CPSIA information can be obtained
at www.ICGtesting.com
Printed in the USA
BVHW071105100820
585957BV00001B/95

9 781732 870475